The Possible Lives of WH, Sailor

Above all, for my mother Adassa Gabbidon Junaid, who was born in Dumbarton, St. Ann, Jamaica and lived for 50 years in St. John's, NL; my siblings who grew up there with me—Adiat Fae, Leila, Ayoka, and Richard; and my nephews Nolan and Theo.

~BJ

The Possible Lives of W.H. Sailor

written and illustrated by

Bushra Junaid

FOREWORD

The Possible Lives of WH, Sailor grew out of the exhibition *What Carries Us: Newfoundland and Labrador in the Black Atlantic,* which was presented at The Rooms Provincial Art Gallery in St. John's from February 29 to September 7, 2020. As a Newfoundlander of African and Caribbean background, I am grateful to The Rooms for the opportunity to bring an African-diasporic perspective to Newfoundland and Labrador's centuries-long place in global migration and trade relationships. The exhibition revolved around Black-British philosopher Paul Gilroy's concept of "The Black Atlantic"—a term that describes the cultural and other contributions of African-descended people to societies on both sides of the Atlantic Ocean. It also reflected on and was presented alongside British-Ghanaian artist John Akomfrah's *Vertigo Sea* (2015), an epic media artwork about humanity's relationship to the sea and its place in the history of migration, conflict, and slavery. The exhibition included works by several Canadian artists (Sandra Brewster, Shelley Miller, Camille Turner) and one British artist (Sonia Boyce), as well as historical items from The Rooms Collection. Amongst the items in the collection were the remains of a 19th-century sailor, discovered on the Labrador Coast in the late 1980s, referred to as WH. In his book *Black Jacks: African American Seamen in the Age of Sail* historian W. Jeffrey Bolster wrote about the little-known but significant role Black people played in all manner of seafaring, including on naval, fishing, whaling, and privateering voyages, as riverboat men, and as translators. Ever since I have been taken by WH and the part Black sailors played in advancing ideas of democracy and freedom.

I don't know your rightful name,

And I don't know from whence you came—

All I know is it's a shame

That there's no one to claim

Your remains.

I don't know from whence you came,

And I don't know your rightful name,

But it's time that you

Were laid to rest again.

Some may say I've got no skin in the game,

Yet if it's really all the same,

This child of the diaspora would like to claim

You as kin.

Coastal erosion takes the blame

For making your two-hundred-year-old coffin plain.

Buried with your head oriented east,

Toward Africa to face your Maker in peace,

Laid to rest on the Strait of Belle Isle,

You were young and short in stature;

Missing your forearm, for that matter.

Was this the factor

That led to your demise?

Your kinky hair and strong teeth,

Your knife, the shoes on your feet,

The clothes that you wore—

All are clues to who you were,

And the customs to which you bore

Witness.

Can your bones tell us more?

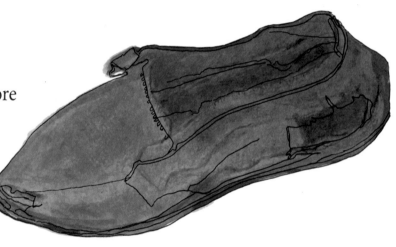

Initials were carved into your shoe, knife, and pouch.

What truths would you utter from your mouth

If you could tell us your story,

Something of your history?

We'll never know how you were maimed,

Or on which ship you came.

Maybe what was unearthed will give birth

To a renaming, a reclaiming of dignity and worth.

I will place a marker near the site

Where you lost your fight, and

Let it stand for all the Black fathers and brothers who plied these waters,

For all the unnamed mothers and daughters bound to plantations,

To suffer cruel trials and tribulations,

Fuelling that trade in

        salt fish sugar molasses rum human beings

For centuries upon centuries to come.

I will give you the dignity and respect you deserve;

Give us a voice to be heard—

For it's time for you

To be laid to rest again.

What did you see

As you travelled sea to shining sea,

Passing icebergs and fjords,

Rocky beaches and craggy shores,

Towering waves, shipwrecks, drownings?

Pulse racing, heart pounding,

Were you awestruck by the mystery,

By the sights and sounds of natural and human history:

Egrets, gulls, seabirds, shoals of fish, seals, polar bears, porpoises,

humpbacks, killer whales,

Sharks, navigating the immensity?

Did the depth and darkness of the oceans and the ever-changing sky mesmerize you,

As dugout canoes, punts, schooners, fishing boats, whaling ships, sail boats, steamboats,

Conveyors of people and goods, charted their way through

The waters blue?

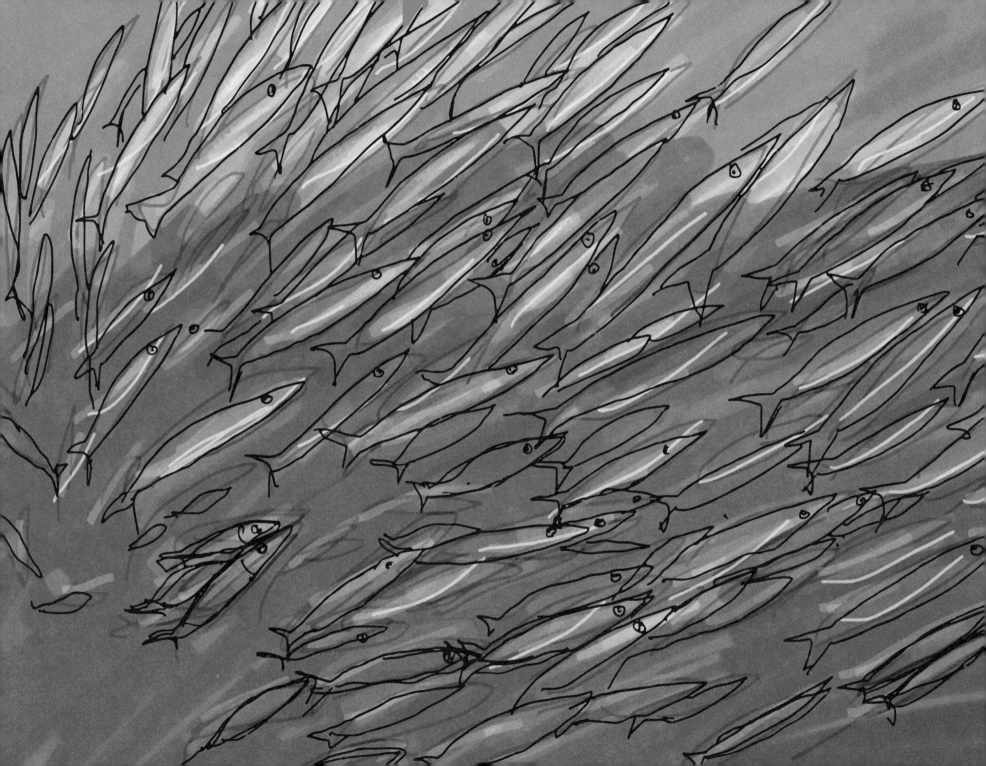

The sights, the sounds of nature's bounty juxtaposed with those

Of fishing, sealing, whaling, hunting, seafaring and other human deeds,

Captains steering vessels, shipmates furling and unfurling sails,

fishermen pulling codfish-

Laden nets with ease

What was the land of your birth?

Do you remember the colour and smell of its earth?

Were you born on West African soil,

Captured as a child and sold into slavery's toil,

Forcibly transported to the New World in the hold of a slave ship,

That horrendous Middle Passage trip?

Do you remember the wails and the cries,

So much agony, so many lives

Lost?

    And did you cling to the memory of your mother's eyes,

Her scent, her caress, her laughter, her smile?

And what did you carry with you?

Or were you born on a plantation in the Caribbean or the American south?

Did you cut sugarcane, pick cotton, plant rice, through heavy rains, heat, and drought?

Did you make your escape,

Attempt to get out,

By enlisting as a sailor in the British or American navy?

Must have taken a lot of courage and grit.

Did you learn to live by your wits,

And did you know how to lead with your fists?

Or did you hail from much closer—

Perhaps a son of Nova Scotia,

Whose parents fought for England in the American Revolutionary War,

Promised land on its distant, rocky shores,

Only to be given plots that were lifeless and poor?

Did you fight in a battle like Trafalgar?

And what was your experience of war?

Did you fear for your life when the ship came under fire,

Did you say a prayer as things became dire,

Until victory was gained; your opponents, slain?

And did you hear of the Haitian Revolution?

Were you buoyed by this successful rebellion

Of slaves against colonial power:

The first Black republic in the world—freedom flowered!

And did you learn to read and write,

To decipher maps, use navigational instruments and tools, let your imagination take flight?

Did the ship's captain take a shine to you,

Let you hang out with the officers as they dined too?

Did you have special status with the crew?

Did they discriminate or did they give you your due?

Were you a free man or enslaved,

As you traversed the ocean waves?

Did you learn to play an instrument? Could you sing?

Did you gain skills like cutting hair, cooking, carpentry, or boxing in the ring?

Did you carry ideas of democracy and freedom?

Ideas shared with your plantation-bound Black brothers and sisters when you

Encountered them?

Did you father children?

A son? A daughter?

Perhaps you have living relatives, descendants

Who don't know what they're missing.

All these things we can't possibly know—

They have only made my curiosity grow

About all the possible lives you may have lived.

I don't know from whence you came,

And I don't know your rightful name, but you

Remain.

Respect is due. It's time that you

Were laid to rest anew.

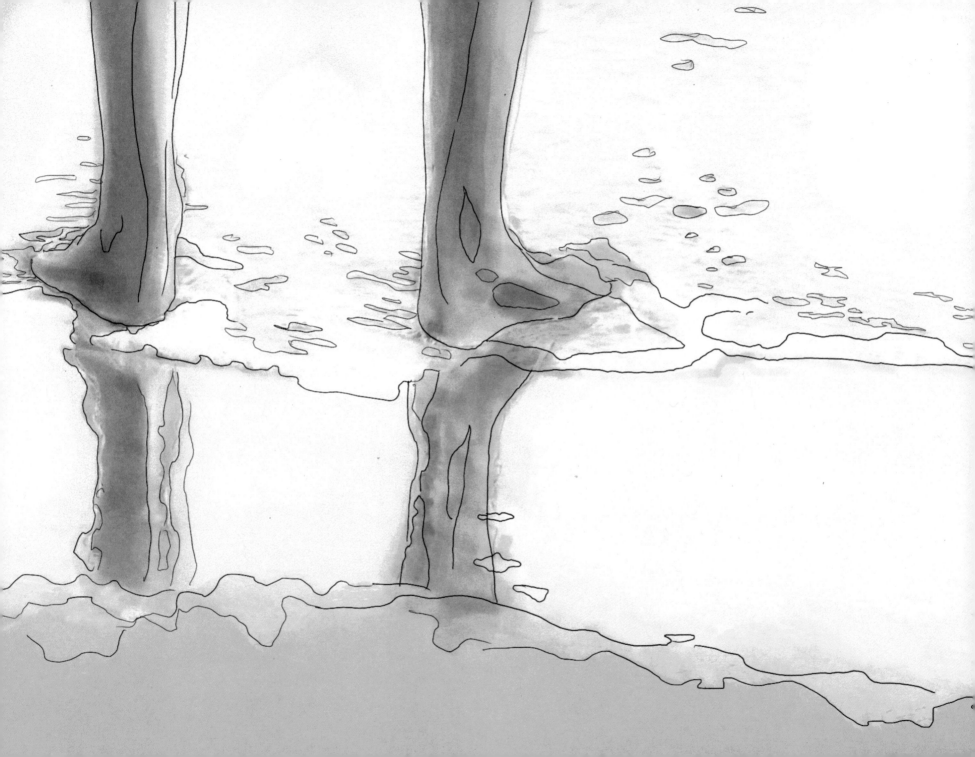

Background: Finding WH

In 1987, an eroding cliff in the area of the Labrador coast called the Strait of Belle Isle, near the small fishing village of L'Anse au Loup, revealed a burial site in the sandy soil outside of the town cemetery. Passersby had seen bones, fabric, and wood sticking out of the ground, so an archaeologist, James Tuck, was asked to investigate. A coffin was unearthed, and the lid was removed. Inside it, a skeleton was lying on top of soft woolen padding; a wool blanket was tucked around it and wrapped snuggly around its head.

An osteologist (a specialist in studying old bones) and a conservator, both from the Memorial University of Newfoundland in St. John's, were asked to examine the skeletal remains and the personal belongings buried with them, which included a jacket, trousers, and shoes.

The experts studied the skeleton and a sample of the hair, and decided the remains were of a young Black man, who was about 22 years old when he died. The young man was short, and was also missing a forearm, which they believe may have been the cause of his death. His teeth were in excellent condition, without any cavities, suggesting that he had had a good diet.

The initials "WH" were carved into his knife handle and "W" was carved in the sole of one of his shoes. Other things found in the coffin included: a loose key in the trouser pockets; a fur hat; a waistband, a knee-length stocking, and a twenty-centimeter-long wooden marlinspike (a pointed tool that sailors use to separate or join together strands of rope).

After analyzing his clothing, the experts decided he was probably a sailor. All these clues together made the researchers think that "WH" may have been a midshipman, a lower-ranking officer, or a servant to a ship's officer, and that he died and was buried in the early 1800s.

This would not be unusual. Roughly one-fifth of American and British seamen in the early 19th century were Black, and the first six English-language autobiographies written by Black people were of seamen describing their lives and experiences. WH reminds us of the role Black people had in shaping the Atlantic world through their involvement in all manner of seafaring, including on naval, fishing, whaling, and privateering voyages, and as riverboat men and translators. Black sailors like WH carried news of war, revolution, the sights and sounds of distant lands, and ideas of democracy and freedom to Blacks enslaved on plantations.

Who was "WH"? Where was he born? Where did he grow up? Who were his people? What was his life like? How did a young Black sailor end up buried in a place that was likely far away from his home?

We may never know the answer to any of these questions, but we can paint a picture of what the life of a Black sailor in the late eighteenth or early nineteenth centuries may have been like from the historical accounts of other sailors.

***

In developing this work, I drew from C. Mathias and S. M. Jerkic's article "Investigating 'WH': A Nineteenth Century Burial from L'Anse au Loup" and W. Jeffrey Bolster's *Black Jacks: African Seamen in the Age of Sail.* Both sources are included in the book's resources and references.

BACKGROUND TO TIMELINE

The Possible Lives of WH, Sailor imagines the life of a 19th-century Black sailor whose remains were discovered buried on the Labrador Coast in the late 1980s. The kind of life WH may have lived—where he may have come from and what he may have experienced or witnessed on his travels—is contemplated in this book.

WH lived during the era of the transatlantic slave trade, which spanned the 16th to 19th centuries, and involved the abduction and enslavement of some 15 million or more African men, women, and children. Carried in horrific conditions in the holds of boats—a journey known as the Middle Passage during which many perished—these Africans carried their histories, memories, languages, foodways, cultures, and spiritual beliefs with them to the New World.

Newfoundland and Labrador, like other communities along the Atlantic, was drawn into what was known as "The Triangle Trade." Nineteen slave ships were built on the island of Newfoundland in order to transport this human cargo, sailing to West Africa with rum and other goods to trade for African captives. The vessels returned with the captives who would be sold to plantation owners in North and South America and the Caribbean. The boats then carried the products of enslaved labour, such as cotton, sugarcane, sugar, rum, and molasses, to sell in Newfoundland and Labrador, Europe, and other markets.

Caribbean slave owners bought enormous quantities of the poorest grade of Newfoundland and Labrador's salted codfish or "salt fish" (also called "refuse fish" or "Jamaica fish") to feed their enslaved workforce. These slave owners were important customers who were vital to Newfoundland and Labrador's economy. In a 1791 debate on whether to abolish the slave trade, British parliamentarians were warned that Newfoundland's fishery would collapse "if it were not for the vast quantity of inferior fish bought up for the West Indian slaves which was quite unfit for any other market." [1]

The slave trade was abolished in the British Empire in 1807. Slavery itself was abolished in 1834.

---

[1] Mr. Alderman Watson in *The debate on a motion for the abolition of the slave-trade: in the House of Commons on Monday and Tuesday, April 18 and 19, 1791, reported in detail,* 2d ed. (London: Printed by J. Phillips, 1792), 112.

TIMELINE

1497:	Italian explorer John Cabot arrives off the coast of Bonavista, NL and "discovers" the "New World"
1526 – 1867:	The Transatlantic Slave Trade is on-going
1583:	Sir Humphrey Gilbert takes possession of Newfoundland for Elizabeth I
1608:	First recorded Black person in Canada—Mathieu DaCosta, a free man hired as an interpreter for Samuel Champlain's 1605 expedition
1619:	First enslaved Black people arrive at Jamestown
1628:	First recorded Black resident of New France—Olivier La Jeune
1709:	Louis XIV authorizes slavery in New France
April 19, 1775 - September 3, 1783:	The American Revolutionary War
1783-1785:	Black Loyalists (Black people who sided with those loyal to Great Britain during the American Revolutionary War) arrive in Canada
1789:	Publication of *The Interesting Narrative of the Life of Equiano, or Gustavus Vassa, The African*, the memoir of an African sailor.
1790:	Imperial Statute allows enslaved people to be brought into Canada
August 22, 1791- January 1, 1804:	The Haitian Revolution

1792:	1200 Black Nova Scotians leave Halifax because of discrimination and harsh living conditions to relocate to Sierra Leone
1793:	Upper Canada Lieutenant Governor John Graves Simcoe's Anti-Slave Trade Bill
October 21, 1805:	The Battle of Trafalgar
March 25, 1807:	George III signs the Act for the Abolition of the Slave Trade in the British Empire; while this act outlawed the transportation of slaves from Africa, slavery itself was still legal and those already enslaved remained so.
September 18, 1812 – February 18, 1815:	The War of 1812
September 1813- August 1816:	2000 Black refugees fleeing enslavement in the United States set sail for Nova Scotia
1815-1865:	The Underground Railroad aids tens of thousands of African Americans who seek refuge in Upper and Lower Canada
August 1, 1834:	Abolition of Slavery in the British Empire
1845:	Publication of the first edition of *Narrative of the Life of Frederick Douglass, an American Slave*
1912:	Publication of *A Negro Explorer at the North Pole: The Autobiography of Matthew Henson*
1987:	Remains of Black seaman, WH, found on the Labrador coast. Analysis determines that the remains date from the early 1800s.

REFERENCES AND RESOURCES

For a more detailed outline of the Black experience in Canada and related histories check out:

WEBSITES

- African Americans and Whaling: https://americanhistory.si.edu/on-the-water/fishing-living/commercial-fishers/whaling/african-americans
- African American Naval History: https://www.history.navy.mil/browse-by-topic/diversity/african-americans/chronology.html
- Black Sailors in the Age of Sail: https://shiphistory.org/2021/02/05/black-sailors-in-the-age-of-sail/
- Britain's Black Sailors: https://www.liverpoolmuseums.org.uk/black-history-month/britains-black-sailors
- BBC 4 – The Extraordinary Equiano 2005: https://youtu.be/zQaF4BNY9LA (A resource for educators or more sophisticated learners)
- Canadian Encyclopedia: https://www.thecanadianencyclopedia.ca/en/timeline/black-history
- Historica Canada—Black History in Canada Education Guide: http://education.historicacanada.ca/files/19/EN_BlackHistory_Digital.pdf
- National Maritime Historical Society—Sea History for Kids: https://www.seahistory.org/kids/
- Teaching African Canadian History: https://teachingafricancanadianhistory.weebly.com/
- Transatlantic Slave Trade Database: https://www.slavevoyages.org/

BOOKS AND ARTICLES
(titles with asterisks are for younger readers)

- *Aronson, Mark and Marina Budhos. *Sugar Changed the World: A Story of Magic, Spice, Slavery, Freedom and Science.* NY: Clarion Books, 2010.
- *Bello, Bayyinah. Kervin Andre (illustrator). *Sheroes of the Haitian Revolution.* MD: Thorobred Books, 2019.
- Bolster, W. Jeffrey. Black Jacks: *African American Seamen in the Age of Sail.* Cambridge, MA: Harvard University Press, 1998.
- Cooper, Afua. *The Hanging of Angelique: The Untold Story of Canadian Slavery and the Burning of Old Montreal.* NY: HarperCollins, 2006.
- *Derenoncourt Jr, Frantz. *Haiti: The First Black Republic.* MD: Thorobred Books, 2021.
- Douglass, Frederick. *Life and Times of Frederick Douglass, Written By Himself: His Early Life As a Slave, His Escape From Bondage, and His Complete History.* 1892; NY: Penguin Random House, 2000.
- Equiano, Olaudah. *The Interesting Narrative of the Life of Olaudah Equiano.* 1794; NY: Modern Library, 2004.
- *Equiano, Olaudah. Adapted by Ann Cameron. *The Kidnapped Prince: The Life of Olaudah Equiano.* NY: Puffin, 2005.
- Henson, Matthew. *A Negro Explorer at the North Pole.* 1912; Berkeley, CA: West Margin Press, 2021.
- Hill, Lawrence. *The Book of Negroes.* Toronto: HarperCollins, 2011.
- Kurlansy, Mark. *Cod: A Biography of the Fish that Changed the World.* 1997; Toronto: Vintage Canada, 1998.
- *Kurlansky, Mark. S.D Schindler (illustrator). *A Cod's Tale.* London: Puffin Books, 2014.
- Mackey, Frank. *Done with Slavery.* Montreal: McGill-Queen's University Press, 2010.
- *Maddison-MacFadyen, Margot. Yvonne Soper (illustrator). *Mary: A Story of Young Mary Prince: Sold at a slave auction and afraid for her life, she runs away.* Hunt River, PEI: Sisters Publishing, 2017.
- Mathias, C. and S.M. Jerkic. "Investigating 'WH': A Nineteenth Century Burial from L'Anse au Loup." In *Labrador–Canadian Journal of Archaeology / Journal Canadian d'Archeolgie.* Vol 19 (1995) pp 101-16.
- *Myers, Walter Dean. Floyd Cooper (illustrator). *Fredrick Douglass: The Lion Who Wrote History.* NY: HarperCollins, 2017.
- Prince, Mary. *The History of Mary Prince: A West Indian Slave Narrative.* Mineola, NY: Dover, 2004.

- *Rappaport, Doreen. London Ladd (illustrator). *Frederick's Journey: The Life of Frederick Douglass.* NY: Little, Brown and Company, 2015.
- *Sadlier, Rosemary. Qijun Wang (illustrator). *The Kids Book of Black Canadian History.* Toronto: Kids Can Press, 2010.
- Whitfield, Harvey Amani. *North to Bondage: Loyalist Slavery in the Maritimes.* Vancouver: UBC Press, 2016.

ART

- Akomfrah, John. "Vertigo Sea" (2015).
- Junaid, Bushra. "What Carries Us: Newfoundland and Labrador in the Black Atlantic" (2020). Https://www.therooms.ca/exhibits/past-exhibit/what-carries-us-new-foundland-and-labrador-in-the-black-atlantic
- Miller, Shelley. Trade (2020). http://tradeproject.shelleymillerstudio.com/

ARTIFACTS FOUND AT WH's BURIAL SITE

Leather shoe from L'Anse Au Loup Burial
(Photo and collection of The Rooms, St. John's, NL)

Initial "W" on bottom of shoe from L'Anse Au Loup Burial (Photo and collection of The Rooms, St. John's, NL)

Leather pocket or pouch from L'Anse Au Loup Burial
(Photo and collection of The Rooms, St. John's, NL)

Initials "W.H." on knife handle from L'Anse Au Loup Burial
(Photo and collection of The Rooms, St. John's, NL)

Teachers are encouraged to read the text aloud or have students do so.

The suggested questions in terms of geography, history, social studies, science, and English relate to the text or offer possibilities for further study. Teachers may wish to choose from or adapt them, depending on the age group of students.

- Read the autobiography of a 19th-century Black sailor. What was their life like? How did their life as a sailor differ from that of a Black person enslaved on a plantation? (Some possibilities: Olaudah Equiano, Frederick Douglass, Matthew Henson)
- What types of seafaring roles did Africans have before and during the transatlantic slave trade?
- What types of vessels would a 19th-century seaman sail on or witness? How were they constructed and for what purpose? What were some technological innovations in shipbuilding over the centuries and what did they make possible? How did advances in foodstuffs, and their handling and storage, impact ocean voyages?
- What was life like for 19th-century sailors aboard a ship? What different kinds of roles did the crew have on ships?
- What types of sea life and animals might a sailor see?
- Were you surprised to learn of the role that Newfoundland and Labrador played in the transatlantic slave trade? How does this change your world view?
- The writer asks us to consider imaginatively many things about WH. What questions did you find yourself wondering about him?
- Apparently, WH was buried with care and with all his belongings. What do you think this says about the relationship he had with his crew mates and the people in the community where he was buried?
- If you were to erect a monument to commemorate WH's life or the historical Black presence in Newfoundland and Labrador, what would it look like and why? How else might you commemorate WH's life?
- After reading about WH what do you imagine him being like or what qualities do you imagine him having? (For example, adventuresome, homesick)

- How does learning about WH change your view of history/Black history?
- How does WH's presence in Newfoundland and Labrador soil change our understanding of the province's history? About Canada's history?
- In the years since WH was discovered, advances in DNA have allowed scientists to learn much more from historical remains. Using DNA technology what questions may we be able to answer now?
- What were the causes and consequences of the transatlantic slave trade? How did the transatlantic slave trade impact the world? What were some short, immediate, and long-term consequences of the slave trade?
- What are some foodways, skills, cultural and spiritual beliefs enslaved Africans brought with them to the New World? What are some examples of how those foodways, skills, cultural and spiritual beliefs were transformed or endured? What are some current examples of how they continue to evolve or innovate?

ACKNOWLEDGEMENTS

I am deeply grateful to Marnie Parsons, editor and publisher of Running the Goat, for the opportunity to imagine the life of a forgotten 19th-century sailor and bring attention to the intersection of Black history and the history of Newfoundland and Labrador; Veselina Tomova for her creative book design; my dear friend Erica Simmons, historian, for her expertise, advice, and support in so many areas; my lifelong friend Adele Carruthers, for her generosity and support, and for always being there for me and mine; and the many friends and relatives who listened and provided advice and encouragement, including: Barbara Brockmann, Ontario educator, for her feedback and ideas about resources and engaging learners in historical thinking; my nieces Marsha Graham and Caelyn S.O. Graham; Angela Britto; Mark Haslam; Eleanor Hendrickson; Nas Khan, Ontario educator; Kim Marson; Sarah Power; the Simmons/Levin family; and many others; and to Leah Snyder, Elijah Garrard, Kristine Buerano, and, in particular, Jessica De Vittoris, for technical/production assistance.

This book was designed by Veselina Tomova of Vis-à-vis Graphics, St. John's, NL, and printed in Canada.

Running the Goat, Books & Broadsides gratefully acknowledges support for its publishing activities
from Newfoundland and Labrador's Department of Tourism, Culture, Arts and Recreation through its Publishers Assistance Program;
the Canadian Department of Heritage through the Canada Book Fund; and the Canada Council for the Arts,
through its Literary Publishing Projects Fund.

Newfoundland
Labrador

Canada Council   Conseil des arts
for the Arts   du Canada

Funded by the Government of Canada
Financé par le gouvernement du Canada   Canadä

Running the Goat
Books & Broadsides Inc.
General Delivery/54 Cove Road
Tors Cove, Newfoundland and Labrador A0A 4A0
www.runningthegoat.com